curious about

BIRDS

T0004775

BY JILL SHERMAN

AMICUS · AMICUS INK

What are you

curious about?

CHAPTER THREE

Playing with Your Bird

PAGE

16

Curious About is published
by Amicus and Amicus Ink
P.O. Box 227
Mankato, MN 56002
www.amicuspublishing.us

Editor: Alissa Thielges
Series Designer: Kathleen Petelinsek
Book Designer: Ciara Beitlich
Photo researcher: Bridget Prehn

Library of Congress Cataloging-in-Publication Data
Names: Sherman, Jill, author.
Title: Curious about birds / by Jill Sherman.
Description: Mankato : Amicus, [2021] | Series: Curious
about pets | Includes bibliographical references and index.
| Audience: Ages 6–9 | Audience: Grades 2–3
Identifiers: LCCN 2019053824 (print) | LCCN 2019053825
(ebook) | ISBN 9781681519692 (library binding) | ISBN
9781681526164 (paperback) | ISBN 9781645490548 (pdf)
Subjects: LCSH: Cage birds—Juvenile literature.
Classification: LCC SF461.35 .S54 2021 (print) |
LCC SF461.35 (ebook) | DDC 636.6/8—dc23
LC record available at https://lccn.loc.gov/2019053824
LC ebook record available at https://lccn.loc.gov/2019053825

Photos © Shutterstock/Eric Isselee cover, 1, 6 (Amazon), 8, 21
(caique); Shutterstock/Christina Marie Saymansky 2 (left), 9;
Shutterstock/Tracy Starr 2 (right), 15; Shutterstock/Lisa Eastman
3, 18–19; iStock/luxiangjian4711 5; iStock/MediaProduction
6–7 (grey); 123rf/Bonzami Emmanuelle 6–7 (Monk);
Shutterstock/Tap10 7 (ringneck); Shutterstock/Evelyn D. Harrison
10–11; Dreamstime/Milkovasa 12–13; iStock/igeldowsett 14;
Shutterstock/binoyphotofolio 17; 123RF/Chee Siong The 20;
Shutterstock/cynoclub 21 (cockatiel and African grey), Jagodka 21
(budgerigar), LM Photos 21 (Quaker); Pixabay/gdakaska 22–23

Printed in the United States of America

Why do pet birds sing?

Tweet! Trill! Cheep! Chirp! Wild birds sing to talk to each other. They may sing to defend their **territory** or find a **mate**. Pet birds sing to communicate, too. They sing to their owner or other birds. Some birds have special songs to greet people. And some birds just sing or whistle to show off.

Macaws are the biggest and loudest pet birds.

NOISE LEVELS

QUIET
Finches
Female Canaries
Doves

CHATTER
Budgies

WHISTLE/SING
Cockatiels
Male Canaries

SQUAWK
Macaws
Conures
Parrots

Can all pet birds talk?

HOW MANY WORDS CAN A PARROT LEARN?

Amazon: 300 words

African Grey: 1,000 words

No. Only parrots can. They **mimic** human words. But you can't really have a conversation. They copy sounds that they hear often. Those sounds may be words. But they can also copy other birds, telephones, or doorbells!

Monk: 60 words

Indian Ringneck: 250 words

Why do pet birds click their beaks?

A bird may click its beak to greet you.

Beak clicking means your bird is content. Birds make this noise by snapping their beaks closed with each breath. They do it because they are happy. A pet bird might also click its beak to ask to be held.

DID
YOU KNOW?
**Birds can wag their tails,
just like dogs. It means they
are happy.**

Why do birds pick at their feathers all the time?

Clean feathers are important to a bird's health.

This is called **preening**. Birds like to stay clean. They stroke and straighten their feathers. They use their beak to remove dust, dirt, and bugs. They also spread oil around. The oil comes from a **gland** on their tail. It keeps their feathers healthy.

Will my bird lay an egg?

A female may make a nest before laying an egg.

Maybe! Female birds sometimes lay eggs. This is normal. But it doesn't mean a baby chick is on the way. Was your bird around a male bird recently? If not, the egg will not hatch. There is no baby bird inside. It is safe to throw it away.

Head twisting is a playful move.

Do pet birds get bored?

Yes. Pet birds are very smart and **social**. They get bored if they are ignored. They need toys to keep busy. Some birds like food puzzles. Keep it exciting. Swap in new toys every so often. Spend time with your bird and hold it every day. You can even teach it tricks!

Parrots like to hang upside down while playing.

Can I pet my bird?

It depends on the bird. Some don't mind a gentle pet. Parrots like head scratches. Some birds don't like being touched. They just want to be around you. Others may not be used to your touch. If a bird wants a pet, it will bow its head toward you. That means, "Scratch here, please!"

This bird enjoys having
its head scratched.

Can a bird be let out of its cage?

Pet birds and dogs can learn to be friends.

Yes. Birds love to be out of their cages. They can stretch their wings. You are a part of your bird's **flock**. Get to know your bird. Just make sure all outside doors and windows are closed. Pet birds shouldn't be let outside. They could fly away and get lost.

How do I know if my bird is upset?

Head feathers can raise when a bird is upset.

Are its feathers ruffled? Is its tail flared? Are its **pupils** small? These are signs that a bird is scared or angry. Be careful. It may bite.

Birds like routine. Keep your bird happy by sticking to a schedule. Feed them at a set time. When you are away, give them a toy to play with.

COCKATIEL

BUDGERIGAR

AFRICAN GREY

QUAKER

CAIQUE

ASK MORE QUESTIONS

I want a bird. What breed would be best for me?

How long do birds live?

Try a BIG QUESTION: How do I bond with my bird?

SEARCH FOR ANSWERS

Search the library catalog or the Internet.
A librarian, teacher, or parent can help you.

Using Keywords
Find the looking glass.

🔍

Keywords are the most important words in your question.

❓

If you want to know about:

- different kinds of birds, type: PET BIRD BREEDS

- how long an African grey parrot lives, type: AFRICAN GREY PARROT LIFE SPAN

FIND GOOD SOURCES

Here are some good, safe sources you can use in your research.
Your librarian can help you find more.

Books

My Pet Bird
by Barry Cole, 2019.

Pet Birds: Questions and Answers
by Christina Mia Gardeski, 2017.

Internet Sites

Animal Planet | Pets 101: Birds
https://www.animalplanet.com/tv-shows/pets-101/videos/parrots
Animal Planet has educational TV shows about animals.

Wild Pets at the Vet: Macaws and Other Pet Birds
https://kids.nationalgeographic.com/videos/wild-pets-at-the-vet/
National Geographic explores the planet. It is a good source for animals and nature.

Every effort has been made to ensure that these websites are appropriate for children. However, because of the nature of the Internet, it is impossible to guarantee that these sites will remain active indefinitely or that their contents will not be altered.

SHARE AND TAKE ACTION

Go birdwatching.
See local bird species in the wild.

Make a bird feeder.
Hang it somewhere wild birds can find it and watch them eat it.

Learn about the threats to wild birds.
How can you help? Share what you've learned with others.

GLOSSARY

flock A group of birds.

gland An organ in the body that makes chemicals and releases a substance or smell.

mate One of a breeding pair of animals.

mimic To copy.

preen To make yourself look good by cleaning and grooming your body.

pupil The black part of the eye.

social Friendly and liking to be around others.

territory The area an animal considers to be his or her home.

INDEX

About the Author

Jill Sherman is a children's book author living in Brooklyn, New York. She has a pet dog named Reed, whom she spoils endlessly. Reed prefers cuddling on the couch to playing at the dog park, and Jill is perfectly happy with that.